Battling our

Core Fears

Mark F. Kailing, PsyD

Battling our Core Fears

First published in 2016 by LaDena Kailing

Copyright © 2016

ISBN-13: 978-1530644193

ISBN-10: 1530644194

"This book is dedicated to my fellow philosophers, from whom humanity has been continually tutored. Much of my contribution is simply integrating their astounding discoveries. I also salute those precious few who continually seek truth no matter the cost—your courage gives humanity dignity and purpose, as well as hope." -Dr. Mark Kailing

Foreward

Imagine you are sitting in a small lecture room listening to profound ideas about human nature and how to effectively strengthen every area of your life. These deep topics are taught in an environment of love and concern for you. They are explained so simply that you are able to come to your own conclusion about each subject quickly. That is what the Self Mastery Lecture Series is.

This book is one of several from the Self Mastery Lecture Series, transcribed from recordings taken in 2011. Mark Kailing battled cancer during that time, but continued his weekly lectures. Dr. Kailing was a Psychologist for 16 years serving clients in California, Nevada and Utah. He loved to teach. During his education a professor taught him, "You don't truly understand something until you can explain it simply". This led Mark to develop simplified theories on life, personality, the universe, truth, core fears and more. His ability to make the profound simple is what made him a great teacher and leader. Dr. Kailing lectured to thousands of students and clients over the years. His self-mastery lecture series was one of his greatest accomplishments. He always lectured with a big smile on his face and spark in his eye. He was inspired by those who also desired to grow and improve in life.

Dr. Kailing passed away on May 21, 2013 after battling cancer for three and a half years. His example and influence have been felt by countless family, friends, clients, and colleagues. At the time of his death, he and LaDena had been married for 21 years and were raising their five children, Andrew (16), Aubrielle (15), Ammoriah (12), Ava (8) and Amari (4) in a home filled with adventures and love.

Reviews

"I have attended Mark's Self-Mastery lectures for over four months. His testimony, insights and philosophies have expanded my perspective and strengthened me so much it is difficult for me to express." Tex Keen, Mendon, UT

"I was only able to attend one of Mark's lectures, but it changed a portion of my life forever." Jenn Morris, Logan UT

"Simply put, Dr. Mark saved my life. Everyone should read these books. Not only read them, but really think about the magnitude of what is being said. Try to apply it in your life. The results will speak for themselves. I knew Mark and greatly miss our conversations. These books are his voice now...listen to him." Curtis Bankhead, Logan, Utah

"Mark's words are truly inspired! Each paragraph is so profound, I have learned so much! Thank you, thank you, thank you!!!" -Christopher Hostetter, Salt Lake City, UT

A message from LaDena Kailing,

I would encourage you to read this slowly. Take the time to ponder the messages you will read here. You may not agree with all that is shared, but stretch your mind to consider it. You will be glad you did. I've attended this lecture series, and have had deep conversations with Mark about these topics countless times. I'm still learning. I'm still finding little treasures of truth that help me feel excited about my own growth and influence in the world. I hope that happens for you too.

Thank you. I wish you all the best on your path.

Battling our core fears is a big topic.

My first main goal is to motivate you on how important this battle is, so we never make the terrible mistake of avoiding the battle. Then I will share battle strategies for actually winning the battle. So, this first half will be about how serious and dangerous the battle really is, and the second half will be how to win the battle. This topic really could be seen as the purpose of life itself, it is that important. You can measure the success of a person by how nobly they have battled against their core fears. This could be the truest test of a person's character, of a person's integrity, that they look at the battle inside of them and face their weaknesses, insecurities and fears.

For those that believe in a heavenly reward after this life, I don't know of any better measure by which to base our reward off of, than to face our fears and to fight this battle.

Another angle is that science has always affected our view on spirituality and religion. Our modern science is starting to realize that there are dimensions inside of dimensions inside of dimensions. I think this is affecting our view on religions, considering that heaven might be a dimension inside the physical dimension. People are realizing that heaven is not someplace up on Mount Olympus, it's not someplace up in the sky or over on a star. It's a dimension that is possibly inside the physical dimension. So, our ability to access deeply into heaven may be dependent upon how deeply we can go inside of ourselves. If there are fears blocking our exploration of our soul, it may limit how deeply we can access heaven, the eternal dimension inside.

We must be humble in facing our fears in order to go deep into that spiritual dimension. It might be scientifically so, that we can't access deeper spiritual dimensions because we have not opened ourselves deep enough. There is an old myth that many cultures and religions have where there is some great treasure, usually inside of some cave and it is guarded by some type of monster or dragon. The message of these stories is telling you that the cave is you, and inside of you are fears like monsters and dragons and if you want to be a true hero you must face the dragons inside of yourself. You cannot access the treasures of life and heaven until you go in there face the dragons and earn it.

If we think that treasure is based on gold and money and what have you, then take a look at

Hollywood. Those rich people are not any happier than anyone else. True wealth and treasure is; liking yourself, being comfortable in your own skin, having a really broad and flexible personality that can really comfortably fit into any situation that comes up in life. The difference between happiness and misery is really just how flexible and broad your personality is. If you fit most situations in life, you are happy. Life feels easy. If your personality has been made narrow and rigid from fear, then in most situations in life you will struggle. You will hurt. You don't fit. You will fail at what you try. You won't attain success, achievement, or friendships as those opportunities are narrow. You are comfortable in few situations. That is what fears can do to us.

Interestingly, if there was an ultimate dragon, monster or devil character, how would that character work?

A devil character would be a spirit. Spirit is made of spiritual energy and intelligence as we've talked about. The only way a spirit can influence you is by putting ideas in your head. A spirit is kind of like a radio transmitter and our brain is the radio receiver. We receive in our mind whatever spiritual energy is being shared. If someone is giving nice, positive energy our mind picks up on it. We think better, we feel happier, and we sit up straighter. The devil character being a spirit, the only way that it could hurt us is not by hurting us physically but the evil energy can put thoughts in our head that cause us to hurt ourselves. Thoughts such as, "You're no good. You can't do that. Nobody likes you. You should just give up", and these types of discouraging messages. Those thoughts would be somewhat powerful, but what would make them a whole lot more powerful is if we were afraid of that thought to begin with. If someone had a fear of being unlovable, it would only take a small whisper, "You are unlovable", and it would really affect that person.

One of the things that fear does to us is that it makes us think in black or white extreme ways. Sometimes when you have a bad day you feel that life sucks and it isn't worth living. Sometimes we discover a weakness about ourselves and then we think there is probably nothing good about us. Some jerk pisses us off and we think that we hate all people.   Fears make us go to these extreme thoughts. We start thinking we know what life is all about based on a few little thoughts.   To really destroy you, the devil character would just need to know what your core fear is. It wouldn't whisper some random thing to you, but rather he would whisper something to you that exposes your core fear and you are going to add a lot of power to that thought.   It is like adding gasoline to the fire and it starts to ruin your life.

What do we do when we have a fear in our body?

If you really study the physiological mechanisms of fear you will discover it is a terrible thing to do to yourself. First of all you dump a bunch of adrenaline into your bloodstream. Adrenaline is poison. Adrenaline makes you age like methamphetamine. If you had cells in a petri dish and dropped a little adrenaline in there the cells will start aging and dying. Our blood provides life-giving energy to the cells of our body. Adrenaline squeezes our muscles so tight that it squeezes blood from the muscles in our limbs. We experience lack of oxygen and lack of energy. We tighten our chest to protect our heart and that restricts our oxygen intake. Breathing requires a relaxed chest to stretch and expand. When we tighten our chest we limit the oxygen our body can receive. Adrenaline limits blood flow and oxygen intake just as your body is going into rapid energy spending. Your heart beats faster, your mind is racing, your muscles are tensing and you are wasting a lot of energy. Your body is making it impossible to make new energy, your digestion stops along with the limited blood flow and oxygen intake. Just as you start expending energy real fast you stop making it.

Perhaps even more important that physical energy, is spiritual energy. What does fear do to spiritual energy? It narrows our mind and we don't notice beauty. Have you ever heard a fearful person say, "It is sure a beautiful day today"? A fearful person can walk by the most beautiful thing and not notice it at all. This is because they are blocking things out, their mind is narrowing, they aren't noticing their five senses. Our senses are a way to take in energy. A fearful person starts to get paranoid. They don't want to talk about God, think about God or anything like that. When we are insecure we have a natural tendency to want to hide from God, from a higher power, from anything spiritual. Spirituality exposes us, you have to be pretty secure to be a spiritual person. Spirituality exposes our vulnerability, our fears and weaknesses. You have to be secure and humble. Fear makes us not want to go to church, or meditate or pray. Fear makes us withdraw socially and we are not able to get any spiritual energy through love and relationships with our people. In every way fear cuts us off from energy. Like a sponge, fear wrings energy right out of us. Most illnesses that we encounter are stress and fear related. Stress is like warfare against our body. This goes back to Adam and Eve. If you read the biblical account, Adam and Eve sinned a little and felt guilt for the first time and that made them afraid. They thought they should hide from God.

They say the number one killer in crisis situations is fear. The first rule in a crisis situation is to calm your fear down, get comfortable so you can think straight. Instead, many people run around like chickens with their heads cut off and they do something foolish. I'll watch shows on TV like "I shouldn't be alive" and I see all of these mistakes the people have made while in crisis. They shoot themselves in the left foot, then they shoot themselves in the right foot.

If there is a devil character who cannot harm us physically but he is very intelligent, he could figure out what your core fear is.

He could figure out your core fear just by analyzing your behavior just like any good psychologist could do. The devil character probably knows our core fears and he is waiting for a weak moment when our core fear is being exposed and then comes a whisper. He'll say, "Nobody loves you. You suck.", or something similar to that. Then our fear takes over and we cut ourselves off from God, we squeeze all the energy out from ourselves.

We basically stress ourselves into a panic attack. The amazing thing about panic attacks, for anyone who has had them before, if you stress yourself into a panic attack it hurts so badly that it is a trauma. You are twice as afraid forever after because now you are afraid of having a panic attack. When people have a specific fear about something, it's interesting to ask "Did that thing actually hurt you, or did your fear hurt you? Did you work yourself into a panic attack?" If someone tells me that they are afraid of dogs because a dog bit them once. I ask them on a scale of one to ten how badly did they bleed and perhaps they didn't bleed at all they only received a small scratch however, they worked themselves up into a panic attack. The enemy to the soul had them. He worked them into a panic attack and they developed a fear of dogs. Maybe back in high school someone noticed a zit on our face and now we are afraid of being judged by people.

Core fears have the power to ruin us not just in our present life but it has the potential to ruin our future, and ruin our happiness. It can ruin our personality by narrowing what personality traits we are capable of. It ruins friendships, and it ruins relationships with our higher power. Franklin D. Roosevelt said once, "There is nothing to fear, but fear itself". I don't think he knew how right he was. He was talking about the economy and if people panic during the recession it could turn into a depression. These words are incredibly wise. There is really nothing to fear in the Universe, except our own fear. People say, "but I could die", to justify their fear. We spend so much time fearing death. Some of the masters have said that the core of all fears is the fear that you might die. Even teens think like this, like the example of the zit, "If Billy from the football team notices I will just die". You can tell unconsciously what is going on in their mind by what they are saying.

Let's take a look at the fear of death.

How many of us have been traumatized by our own death so far? None of us have ever died yet, but we fear it. People who have had the rare experience to have died on the operating table and then come back to life to tell what it was like, almost all universally describe their experience with death as a surprise by how it wasn't a big deal. Some state they didn't even know that they had died. They were standing there wondering why everyone was crying. They don't always recognize their own dead body as they look back to the operating table. We fear death as a terrible thing but it turns out to be nothing. It's nothing. It's an illusion. You didn't die completely, you still exist. In fact you are free from a painful body and a painful world and in that way your experience got better.

This thing called fear can ruin our lives and possibly limit how much of heaven we can let in for all eternity. Fear keeps us from opening our minds, and opening our hearts. I don't think we have reason to fear life. I don't think we have a reason to fear the Devil. We have reason to fear our fear. The only way anything can hurt you in this world is through your fear. Fear is the true enemy. Every bad thing that has ever happened to you, you can count on your fears partly making it happen. It is a hidden enemy.

The ancient Greeks had this great story that has great insight on fears.

The story is Oedipus Rex. Rex means king, so this is a story of King Oedipus. When he was a baby boy and his dad was a macho king.   His dad represented the old Greeks. The old Greeks were kind of arrogant they thought what made a man great is if he could kill a lot of men in battle. You could only go to heaven on Mount Olympus if you could kill a bunch of people because you had big biceps. Oedipus' father killed a lot of people and conquered as many kingdoms as he could.   He comes across a prophetess and he asks her to prophecy something for me. She looks at him and discovers his core fear and then she prophecies that he will cause his worst fear to happen. As an arrogant man his worst fear would be for his son to grow up and kill him, take over his kingdom, be a better king, have the people love him more, will marry the King's wife and be a better lover too. The prophetess really exposed the King's greatest fears.

The King wanted to prevent this from happening to him so he decided to kill his son. He figured the people wouldn't love him if they knew he killed his own son, so he comes up with this rationalization and he cuts his son's foot off, then leaves his baby boy son in the wilderness for the wild beasts to kill him. This is how arrogant men think, "Well, I didn't do it." Before the baby is killed by wild beasts a really nice King and Queen from a neighboring kingdom come along, find the baby, adopt him and raise him to become the King of their country. The two Kings of neighboring countries don't know that they are father and son, they don't know each other. The arrogant King thought the baby had died and didn't realize his son grew up to be a King.

One day they cross paths and for some reason the old King doesn't like the young King and they have words and pretty soon they draw swords and the young King kills the older King not knowing he has killed his father. Back then, if you killed the King then you received everything the King had and the young King gets his father's kingdom. He meets the Queen, an older woman but attractive and they fall in love and get married. He is a beloved King, everyone loves him much more than the previous King. The Queen asks about his foot injury and he shares the story. The Queen realizes that this is her son.

In the ancient Greek religious culture it was a terrible sin to have killed your father and slept with your mother. It is unspeakable in their culture.

King Oedipus has a decision to make. What should he do? This is what we all face when we battle our fears. We can either hide from the fear or accept the fear humbly and nobly. His father chose to hide from his fear and kill anybody that exposes his fear. King Oedipus faces his fear knowing everybody is going to hate him, he will lose his kingdom, and the people might kill him. He goes to his people and confesses his sins. He tells them he is not worthy of his kingdom. To show them his sincerity he tells the people that it was because of his eyes that he got into trouble. He saw the old King and didn't like him so he fought him and killed him. He saw the beautiful Queen and married her. The pride of his eyes, and falling for things of this world were his downfall. He stabs his own eyes. A strange thing happened and instead of hating him the people loved him all the more because he was brave, and faced his fears more nobly than most people would have. The people were touched by this and his story is told to this day as an example of a true hero.

If you look at the Greek civilization they really had two periods; an arrogant period and a more sophisticated period.

In the story of Oedipus Rex the father represents the arrogant period where the measure of a true hero is based on your physical strength and power. The young King Oedipus represents the more mature thinking that a true hero is based upon how well you face the enemy within. The enemy inside of you can destroy you for eternity. It is a much more sophisticated view to fight the inward battle.

The Hindus in India have a great saying to show how little you should worry about your outside enemies, "If you wait by the river long enough, the body of your enemy will float by."

This makes a little more sense if you know that in funerals in India they will burn and float the dead bodies down the river. It is a spiritual rite of passage. What an interesting saying that if you wait long enough the body of your enemy will float by. This thought has really helped me in tough times when I had an enemy and I really wanted to do something about it to get some revenge but I learned to just chill and wait. At some point later there goes that enemy. His dead body didn't float by but he got fired or that person got their comeuppance in some way. We shouldn't focus too much on our external enemies. We need to focus on the internal enemy.

Let me tell you a personal story of how I came to study core fears.

I studied unconscious fears because I had so many to work on. I had a pretty rough and lousy childhood with a lot of fears and trauma. I had two paths, like we all do. As a teen I decided I was going to try and hide from my fear. I desperately did whatever I could to be in with the popular crowd. I tried to treat life like a party and never take anything serious. I tried to buy all the toys so I could say, "Look what I bought. Look at this." I did all the stupid things that people do to try and hide from their true feelings and insecurities. At age twenty I realized what a wasted life that was. I was causing one tragedy after another. I experienced one missed sacred opportunity after another missed sacred opportunity. My life was getting uglier and uglier and I didn't like the person I saw in the mirror. I began to like that person less and less and less. It hit me really hard and I realized that kind of life is not worth living. This was a very scary thought as a young person. I became a hermit. I decided to fight whatever insecurities that I have. I locked myself up with my insecurities. I went to college and studied anything to do with self-mastery. When they asked me what my major was I said, "I don't care. I just want to learn self-mastery and I'll study whatever you have." I studied world religions, yoga, philosophy, meditation, martial arts, and psychology. I just wanted to study and face my fears instead of hiding from them.

This is similar to what King Oedipus did. When he stabbed his eyes out, he locked his attention inside of himself. Our eyes allow us to escape our heart. Instead of focusing on our thoughts and feelings we look around and see something interesting to take our attention. You can distract yourself with your eyes it's as if your spirit, your energy and your attention can leave your body and go somewhere else. King Oedipus locked himself up with his feelings forever.

So, I decided to study and train and not socialize. I realized that most self-mastery techniques do not make much money except psychology, so I became a psychologist. If it were like the ancient Greek times I would've become a philosopher but in our culture the money is in psychology. When I was asked what I wanted to study in psychology I stated, "Anything to do with unconscious fears and defenses". I wanted to learn all of the defensive ways that people hide from their unconscious fear. I wanted to know that stuff like the back of my hand. I became a doctor of psychology and I loved working with this topic. Clients would come into my office I would tell them that we were going to study their core fears and their defenses. If it wasn't for their benefit then it was for mine.

Fortunately, my first job was working at psych hospital. It was a short-term psych hospital so we had a high turnover of people whose lives were destroyed by fears and defenses. We must've had about a hundred people coming through the hospital every week in a busy city (Modesto, California). I had a lot of clients to analyze fears and defenses. I became an expert on this subject. I developed some research studies on how to overcome this system. Originally, my research premise is that there is one deep defense that people have. There is some deep, dark, defense that is interfering with the person's life. I found this to be true with every one of my clients. I started to wonder how that could be true. I found it everywhere I looked. I wondered if there wasn't just one but several fears that affected everything about a human being from the clothes they wear, to the way the speak, to the political party they like, to the religion they chose and to the partner they end up with. I estimated that I've done twenty thousand little tests in a row and I found this every single time.

I did classes for my clients where I challenged them on their core fears. I wanted to do a blind study, where I'm not influencing the study. I would take one client and ask the class something that stood out about that person and we'd discuss what their core fear was based on that outstanding trait. One time the class thought they stumped me they said the thing that stood out about this client was that he was wearing purple tennis shoes. How could purple tennis shoes have anything to do with your core fear? What do the purple shoes symbolically represent? It is kind of a rebellious thing but it's also a passive thing. It's down low where most people wouldn't notice the rest of him was dressed in a conservative fashion. I talked with the client saying, "You want to be a rebel but you are afraid to, so you do it passively. What kind of childhood could've caused that? You wanted to measure up but your family was so perfectionistic that you couldn't. You probably had an older sibling who was a high achiever and always out-doing you. In order to hide from your feelings of not measuring up you became a rebel. Rebellion is just a way of hiding from caring too much instead of trying and risking failure. Your parents were really scary and dominating so you couldn't really rebel too much so you've developed some passive ways of rebelling. You probably played a lot of video games." The client confirmed that I was challenging his core fear of not being accepted.

I got so good at this that for a while I wondered if I might be psychic. I remember going to the grocery story with my wife and I was watching the people in the crowd. I was able to quickly discover the core fears of all of the customers in the store around me and I didn't like it. I was overwhelming to process and to have that information. I came to realize that I'm not psychic I've just come know the core fears so well that they became very easy to spot.

I developed a very simple, little test where you could figure out what anyone's core fear is.

I'm going to teach you how to do it. I can't tell you how many people that this has helped. I typically hear from clients, "I've been in therapy my whole life and no one has been able to tell me what my core fear is." It's a simple equation. This is it. Everything in the Universe has an opposite. If we are afraid of something we are naturally going to do the opposite. You can figure out what someone's fear is because their fear is the opposite of what they are doing. Let me give you an example to help it make more sense. If someone is afraid of aggression, they don't like when people are mad at them, they become a real people-pleaser. They are always eager to please everybody. They are so afraid of aggression that they become very passive.

When you meet someone who is always eager to please everyone now you know that they are afraid of not pleasing others and they are afraid of aggression.

If you think like an artist you can observe what it is that stands out about a person and then figure out what the opposite behavior is. It's human nature to go in the opposite direction of your fear. If there is a lion to my right, you can be sure that I'm going to go to my left. We don't tend to make mistakes when it comes to our fears, I wouldn't accidentally go to my right and bump into the lion. When we perceive something is scary, we will head the opposite way to find a way out.

I call this theory The Pendulum Theory because when we fear something to one side then we will tend to run to the opposite side. The one extreme side is what we are afraid of, and the opposite extreme side is our defense. Whatever stands out about us could be a thought, a behavior, a personality trait, a feeling, it could be anything. If I'm an introvert, always looking inside of myself then I'm afraid of the outside world. The outside world intimidates me so I'd rather spend all of my time inside. It could be a personality trait, if I'm attention seeking I'm afraid of being forgotten, alone, abandoned or rejected.

It may be that the most important question you could ask yourself is; "What stands out about me?" If there is some fear, you are running from something. The wonderful thing is that there is good and beauty on every side. Everything has some good and beauty in it. We should experience life in moderation. What happens is that when we're afraid of one side and go to the opposite extreme it causes a few problems. One is that you are not strong in the side that you are running away from because you've never practiced it. The other problem is that the other side, the one that you are running to, is something you are over-doing, you are an extremist at it. Life requires us to be moderate. Whenever we are extreme at something, even when it is an extreme good, it is unhealthy for you. If the person is really loving and does it to an extreme, it is no good. You will become taken advantage of. You may end up with an abusive spouse, someone who disrespects you and you'll raise kids who will grow up and disrespect you. We don't tend to value the people who are door mats. We value those who are moderate.

Another problem with extremism; avoiding one side and going to the opposite extreme, is how it affects other people. This is that theory called polarization that we've talked about before. Polarization is a phenomenon in psychology that basically says that when you do something extreme, you will push other people to do the opposite extreme to balance you out. Everything in the Universe needs to stay in balance, if there is an action they will be an equal and opposite reaction. If someone were to come in here being the class clown, loud and crazy, we'll all be pushed to the opposite side. We might laugh along for a while but then we'll want him to tone it down because he isn't noticing that we are in a serious, quiet situation. We will become polarized with that joker. If your spouse starts wasting money, spending money like crazy then you will become a penny-pincher. You will be very careful with your money, a real tight-wad because your spouse is polarizing you. Not only are you ruining yourself when you become extreme, but you ruin the people around you because they are being pushed to the opposite extreme.

Watch what happens when we put these two theories together; Pendulum Theory where we run to one extreme, and Polarization where we push people to the opposite of us.

Visualize this, then we'll use some examples to help make it more clear. What happens is, if I'm afraid of the right and Pendulum Theory says I will run to the left but now Polarization says that I'm running to the left I'm going to push people around me to the right. The right is what I was afraid of to begin with. In a way I've just pushed all of these people to play out the side that I'm most afraid of.

Throughout history we've know that people cause their fears to happen. Great masters throughout history, religious masters, philosophy masters have stated that we cause our fears to happen but we didn't know why. Now we know why. If you run from your fear then you will push other people to play out the side that you are running from.

After working in the psych hospital for a few years I came up with a list of the ten core fears. The secret to beating our fears is first, to know what our core fear is. It is usually a theme. It's not a thing, but a theme, that we are most afraid of. It is an idea, that is why the Devil can mess with us on it, he knows the theme and then whispers something scary to us about that theme. Each of us is a little uncomfortable with all of these ten fears. A little bit of fear is not going to mess you up. If you have a moderate fear of something you are not going to cause a big polarization. It is not going to turn into a big catastrophe like the story of Oedipus Rex.

If you have a strong fear, that can ruin your life.

It can cause a major polarization. It will put into motion a system that will cause your fear to happen, not just once but over, and over, and over again. Sigmund Freud saw people causing their fears to happen but he didn't know why or how but he called it the "Repetition Compulsion". It basically says that people are compelled to repeat their fears. In order to really figure out what it is that is going to ruin your life, you need to know which of these ten core fears is the strongest. Whichever fear is the strongest is what you would call your core fear. It is at the core of everything in your life. It is why you are one political party and not the other, why you have your personality, and it's why you like the sports team that you do. I won't say that it's the only factor, but it is the one factor at the core of everything about you.

You learn an immense amount about yourself if you know what your core fear is.

Psychology has discovered that there are three things that you can do when you discover a fear; you can fight, you can flight, or you can accept. I look at this as a dichotomy fight and flight are extreme opposites, accept is somewhere in the middle. Acceptance is not a fear reaction. You are courageously accepting the truth of the situation. Fight and flight are two fear reactions that are ways of hiding from our fear. We tend to believe that fighting is this great, wonderful, noble thing but no, it's what animals do when they are cornered. If you scare an animal it will fight or flight, it is a basic fear reaction. Even a bug will do it. If you grab a bee and squeeze it in your hand it will sting you, it fights back because it is afraid. It doesn't think, "I will existentially accept my death today. I will be one with the Universe. I will now transition to the other side." No, it is a fear reaction to fight or flight. Either of those fear reactions will cause our fear to happen.

The most important thing that you can know about yourself is what your core fear is. I charge clients $100 per/hour to do what you can do for yourself for free right now. You take these ten fears and rate on a scale of one to ten how strongly each one of these scares you. Find out which one is a core fear for you.

Abandonment

Failure

Guilt

Rejection

Death

Vulnerability

Lack of Control

The Unknown

Unfairness

Lack of Resources

The more you look at that one core fear, the more you will realize that it was the thing that caused trouble for you back in high school. It was the reason you had conflict with your boss. It caused issues in your marriage. It caused conflict with your children. You will find a theme in your life connected to your core fear. It is the enemy.

Throughout your history it has been at the core of your problems. I will go through these ten fears.

The number one for most women is ABANDONMENT. Women are relational creatures what they fear most is not having a relationship. What does someone with abandonment fear act like? If you have a fear of being alone what do you do? They work hard at getting attention because they want people to like them. Women worry a lot about what other women will think of them. They become clingy in relationships as they seek reassurance that the person will not abandon them. The other extreme reaction to this fear is to avoid relationships, have a solitary job like a librarian, live alone and get a bunch of cats, then watch relationships on television because they are safer that way. Either one of these reactions, fight or flight, causes the fear to happen. If you have a fear of abandonment and so you do the opposite and smoother somebody you will polarize them and push them to the opposite side. When you smoother someone they want to get away from you. They say in dating that you always want what you can't have. If we chase someone it turns them off. The best thing to do is to be moderate. Don't chase anyone and don't run away.

The number one fear for most men is the fear of FAILURE, a fear of being inadequate. Men are a competitive, conquering creature. We have a fear of not conquering and failing. They don't want to be known as the guy that didn't get the homerun, or the guy that can't bring home the bacon. This person might become a super achiever. They become obsessive, they lift weights at 5:00 a.m., then run to work to try and become the richest guy, then play hard and buy the biggest boat, etc. You've seen men who are so worried about any sign of failure. They stress themselves out. They don't really enjoy life. In a way they are a failure because they missed out on deepening their relationships. They didn't take time to really like themselves. They missed out on important things in life by obsessively running around trying to achieve. They may die early because of a stress-related illness. Another reaction could be to avoid facing this fear, a flight reaction, and go down and drink at the bar every night. They compensate for achievement by trying to get the highest score on a video game. Bars are a bad scene. They are filled with men who have fears of failure, alcohol giving them a false sense of achievement. They are sitting beside women who have a fear of abandonment who believe that if she can get the drunk guy to say that he loves her, then she will win some relationship. Those relationships are pretty toxic.

GUILT is a very strong fear. Using fight or flight, people could just hide from guilt. Modern society created a movement to hide from guilt with a hippie philosophy that allows people to do whatever they want to do. They had an 'anything goes' type of philosophy. Do whatever made you happy. That is an extremist way of hiding from guilt. The other extreme, the fight reaction, is to join a religious group and try to be perfect in every way. Being extremist will screw you up. The healthy thing to do, right in the middle, is to half accept the guilt. Feel moderately bad about the situation. Try to do better but not to beat yourself up over it.

REJECTION fear is not quite the same as abandonment.   You don't care if somebody loves you, the way you do in abandonment fear, with rejection fear you just don't want to be dissed. You don't want it to be obvious that someone doesn't like you. You don't want anyone to put you down. Criticism is something that you take very hard.

A fear of DEATH is something we've already talked about. Similar to a fear of death is a fear of VULNERABILITY.   A lot of people are not afraid of death but they are afraid of pain. They aren't afraid of dying but they don't want a needle stuck in their arm at the doctor's office. Sometimes it's a physical pain, and sometimes it's an emotional pain that they are afraid of. They don't want to be vulnerable, like giving a speech in public, which is a very vulnerable thing to do. They are afraid of being unsafe.

Another fear is not having CONTROL. Some people just like to have a lot of control. It's hard to be married to someone with this fear because they want everything to be within their control. The next fear, is fear of the UNKNOWN it is similar to vulnerability. They like to know everything that is going to happen, "Who is going to be there? What is going to happen first? What are we going to have for dinner?" They want to be able to predict what is going to happen. They tend to freak out when things don't happen according to the things they know. It's scary for them to think that the Universe is full of the unknown.

UNFAIRNESS is a part of life. A fear of being treated unfairly is something we must learn to half accept. Be moderate about it. With this fear people go around spying to make sure everything is fair. It really doesn't matter so much. It is an external battle. The last fear is a fear of not having enough RESOURCES; food, clothing, and shelter. In my experience the older generation have this fear a lot more, the people that have gone through the Great Depression. They are dying off, there are not as many of them anymore. Someone like my grandmother who could not throw a single rubber band away, or the plastic containers that butter came in, she saved every little thing.

These ten fears can ruin your life. They are ticking time bombs in your life. They will go off eventually if you don't find them and accept them. Think about that, they are a ticking time bomb that the enemy has put in your life and it can destroy your life. All you have to do is to be brave enough, honest enough, humble enough to go inside that cave inside of yourself. Close your eyes so you are locked in there, and sit down with that core fear. Don't try and fight it. Don't try and deny it. Don't try and run or hide from it. Sit down and acknowledge it's a part of life and it's okay. Sit there until you get used to it. I call it, "sitting down to have tea with your core fear". It's my way of visualizing that you are not there to fight the core fear. This is a great weapon in winning that battle.

Hopefully you will look at the list of core fears and rate each of them on a scale of one to ten and find out which fear is the strongest for you. Analyze it. Think about all of the times in your history that you've had a little fight or flight going on. You were a little too far this way or that way as you tried to hide from that fear. If we had absolutely no fears at all we would naturally be a moderate human being. Nature is a moderate, comfortable balance. Nature is mostly peaceful, no hurry, no worries. Human beings are the ones running around unnaturally doing extreme things due to fear. If a person had no fear they would be moderate. That is why I asked; "What is it that stands out about a person?" It can be anything. It stands out because it is extreme, not moderate. That means something must've been driving it unnaturally. It is driven by an artificial thing; fear.

This battle is deep.

It is at the core of your happiness now and throughout eternity. The battle is there not to kill us but to teach us. It is an incredibly educational process. After those years in the psych hospital I became determined to beat my own core fears. After several years I realized I hadn't made much progress. I became discouraged because I really wanted to beat these core fears but I sensed that it was impossible. I realized the reason it was impossible for me was because I was trying to fight them. When you fight them, you cause them to happen. I was trying too hard instead of accepting them as a part of life. They are very helpful experiences, like black belt masters beating you in the fight, doing so in order to teach you. Eventually they get a good shot in, and you bow and accept it.

Our fear is really at the core of all our problems, in this life and in the next.

Our core fear is what keeps spiritual energy, God, out of us. Our fears block all of the spirit stuff out. Battling our core fears is not only very important for this life but also for the next. Our reward in the eternities depends upon what level of spiritual energies we can open up to. The true battle in this life is not outside of us, it's inside. It seems evident to me that God, or nature, or the great force, whatever you like to call it, wants problems in this dimension. The world was created with problems, they have been here since the beginning. There will always be plenty of problems in our lives for our learning. The problems outside of us will always be there, if it's not one thing it's another. What matters much more is the eternal battle inside; to free your heart, mind and soul. Whether we live or die, suffer or are happy in this world doesn't matter eternally. It's nice to live a happy life, but it's more important that you fight a good fight. At the end of your life, you lay on your death bed and you can say, "I gave everything I had." It doesn't even matter if you won the battle, but you fought it valiantly.

One of my favorite movies, "Rocky", the first one, is a masterpiece. If you look closely, the metaphor of that story is that we are always in some kind of fight. We are all Rocky. In some of those fights we are really struggling. We are up against the ropes, getting bloodied, and we don't look so good. The moral at the end of the story is; it didn't matter if he won the fight. He didn't win the fight. He didn't care if he won the fight. If you watch closely at the end of the fight you'll see that everyone is looking at the announcer to hear who was pronounced the winner but Rocky is leaving, he has nothing left to prove, he isn't even listening to hear whose name is called because it doesn't matter to him. His goal was to give it hell and prove what kind of man, what kind of human being he was. He wasn't fighting the champion, he was fighting his own laziness, his fears, and all the weaknesses of his personality that had messed up his life. He was sick and tired of hiding from the battle. His goal was to be the first guy to not get knocked out by this champion. The beauty of the story, the reason we got all tearful watching it, is because every single time he got knocked down he climbed the ropes. He was half-dead, he was bleeding, no one thought he could get back up but he did. He did. Pretty soon everyone in that auditorium, instead of rooting on the champion, they started chanting, "Rocky! Rocky! Rocky!"

I think that is how God looks at our battle in life. He doesn't care if we win so much. He has given us many unwinnable battles. Some battles are incredibly hard, some we are born with, some will still be around after we die. We won't win every battle or finish every battle. It doesn't matter if you won. Did you get back up? Did you refuse to stay down and be knocked out? Did you go in there with courage? At the end of your life can you say, "I fought a good fight." If you consider what we are up against, we are up against a mighty champ.

I hope by now you are committed to a life-long process of battle training.

I hope you understand how important this is and you are fired up about battling your core fears. Life is just a gym or a class room, where we learn how to fight the battle. We fight to overcome weaknesses, to build things better. We have to learn the principles for success. You can't win by building your biceps. You win this battle by knowing these principles.

Just about every officer training program in the military, all over the world, throughout history, talks about the three rules of war.

We must know the three rules of war.

Number one is to know your enemy. It is a foolish person who rides to battle without knowing what they are up against. You study the enemy. You send out the reconnaissance. You study the experts. Secondly, you practice ahead of time. You never go into battle without any skills. You train and practice all your skills. You drill, you drill, and you drill. You don't forget your musket back at your tent. You take all your tools and training with you. History is full of battles won by one army because that army was trained. If two armies go up to battle against one another, even when one outnumbers the other, if the smaller army has training they can win. What kind of battle do you want to fight? You want to fight the battle that utilizes all of your training and skills. The third rule of war is to fight wisely. You don't run straight into your enemy's strong hold, you divide and conquer. You apply strategies.

We've discussed what core fears are. We've discussed how the Devil character can whisper affirmations of our fear to us and encourage us to cause our fears to happen. We have a good understanding of who our enemy is. Training for the battle within requires self-mastery skills that you will need to practice every day. It needs an important part of your life. This training is what you take with you when you die. I'll teach you what you should be practicing daily. It's really interesting how overcoming our fears really parallels a real live battle in the field. It is a battle against forces that are attempting to destroy us.

I'll reveal one battle strategy; I try not to look at the enemy in a fearful light because it gives the enemy power. I tend to knock my enemy down to size a little bit and remember that the enemy is there because it is trying to teach me. That enemy is in my life because the Divine allows it to be here. The Divine doesn't do anything unless it's for our own good. The very fact that you believe in a Devil character, Evil energy, or even bad luck or bad karma, if you believe in these things then the Divine power allows those things to be here because they are good for our training. Could we even grow without some battles and challenges in life? Is there any gain without any pain?

One of the ways you can knock the enemy down to size is just trusting that there is a lesson somewhere in the experience. Ultimately it will not destroy us. It will not cause us to cease to exist. Yes, there will be some consequences but just like a parent raises a child some of the consequences will suffer the child, but they are for the child's good. It is the same thing with our Divine Parent. There will be some really hard lessons. You can ask yourself why does the Divine give us such hard lessons and you might come up with the idea that we are really hated or that we are such tough spirits that it takes a hard level of challenges in order for us to learn and grow in this world.

A lot of the masters will say that the battle has to stay even.

Divine fairness would say that good and evil have to stay in equal balance. It wouldn't be fair if one was overpowering the other. If you think about it, if everything has to stay in equal balance then if our spirit is this strong, then our challenges have to be this strong. A lot of masters have said that the more challenges you have in this life, the more impressive your soul is. You can take it as a complement. Those with the challenges of schizophrenia, mental retardation, or any other handicap should be viewed with this in mind. A worldly perspective would consider them weak. In an eternal perspective, the people with the greater challenges are the stronger spirits and deserve our respect.

Other faithful perspectives we could take is to be more positive and less discouraging. If you have a lot of problems in your life a parent out there must really care about you. The parent must be really interested in teaching you. There is a scripture that says, "God chastens who He loves." If you love your child, don't you put more effort into teaching the child? Don't you give the child more rules and supervision? If you don't care about the child you don't invest in them. You are the absent parent and don't even know what is important in the child's life.

Another faithful perspective we could take is to consider what it is we will be doing in the hereafter. If all of this world is to train us, we must be using our training in the future, in the eternities. We are getting leadership training. We are getting world governing training. We are getting battle training. What will be doing in heaven? We'll be governing, fighting, creating, and all kinds of amazing things. We are going to help rule in heaven. That is an incredible honor. Who would deserve such a job? Someone who has trained hard, and how got back up when life kicked them down. If someone had no training in life, they were born with a silver spoon in their mouth and had an easy life would you trust them to govern a universe? Have they really proven themselves? I'm not even sure if I would trust them to feed my cat while I was on vacation.

The second rule of war is to practice before you go into battle. You might call this faith. Faith is a powerful self-mastery technique. It's the ability to stay positive even when life is hopeless. When life is difficult anyone can succumb to the depression but that is the easy way out. To stand up to adversity and say that you don't understand why you are experiencing it but that you know there is a spiritual, higher power and it is wise and loving and you trust it. You trust it.

I hope this is not too sensitive of a topic for me to bring up, but you all know that I've been battling cancer for two years now. Early on in my battle with cancer I made up my mind that even though I could get really discouraged and depressed I will go out praising the higher power and stating; "I trust you. If I live or die, I trust you. It's all good." There is a choice. If you want to die with glory, keep a great attitude. Nothing pisses off the enemy more than facing adversity with a positive attitude. The enemy is called a discourager. You can choose to get discouraged and let the enemy have his way with you, or you can practice faith, practice a positive attitude, and trust that it is all for your training. If we really knew what we were being prepared for we would be happy to endure every difficulty we faced. There is an old prayer that says, "Don't pray for an easy life, pray for strength that you can handle more."

Having a positive attitude is not something that you can just turn on in a moment of crisis.

You have to practice it on a daily basis. You have to wake up in the morning and say, "Bring it on." If you like to pray or meditate, there are two important things to really focus on; morning and night. In the morning you express gratitude and ask for strength for that daily battle. At night you express gratitude and ask to be healed up for the next daily battle. If you've lost some battles, you pray that you can get over it quickly. The greatest warriors in this life have short memories. We need to learn to shake things off, we can't stew on our setbacks, that is exactly what the enemy would want you to do. I try and teach my son, he gets embarrassed at school if someone ever teases him. I teach him to just laugh it off. If you laugh with people they realize you are too secure to mess with. Kids who tease seek people who are sensitive and insecure.

Practice faith every morning. My martial arts instructor taught me to bow twice. He said, "You bow when you step on the mat, and you bow when you leave the mat." When you are bowing as you step onto the mat you are saying, "Thank you for this training I'm about to receive." When you bow as you are leaving the mat you are saying, "Thank you for the training I've just received." We also bowed to our opponent whether we won or they won because it doesn't matter, it was training. It takes a big person to be thankful for a training that exposed weaknesses.

One of the most important battle strategies is to stay comfortable.

Every day you have to practice your ability to keep your body comfortable. When your body is comfortable there are a lot of amazing things going on. You are absorbing a lot of spiritual energy, which empowers you in every way. In the scriptures they talk about the Spirit of God, another name for that is the Comforter. When you are comfortable you are taking in spiritual energy like a sponge. When you are absorbing spiritual energy it is radiating around you like a force field. It keeps out negative energy and thoughts.

The practice of self-comfort is best done through meditation. Meditation is really the art of closing your eyes and making yourself comfortable. Try relaxing muscles, breathing better, clearing your mind, or one of many other ways to get comfortable. There are more advanced ways that I can teach you, we'll have another class on that. For now, take a little time every single day to close your eyes and bliss out on comfort. A nice little technique is to go through your five senses and see how deeply you can enjoy each one. Imagine looking out at nature and seeing it like you are a kid at Christmas, like you are seeing nature for the first time. See it in the most beautiful perspective as you can. Get the 'Wow Factor' going. You'll bring in a lot of spiritual energy if you can open your mind and open your heart. Do this with each of your senses and see how magnificent the experience really is. Take a divine perspective on it as much as you can. Everything in nature is spiritual energy, you are swimming in it. The more you can appreciate it, the more you can take in.

The next thing to practice is detachment.

This is an Eastern philosophy. Detachment is misunderstood by the world. You know me, I'm a moderate. In order to truly understand something I have to balance an opposite perspective. Pure detachment is not good. Pure detachment is letting go of all of the world. The opposite would be to rejoice over every single thing, enjoying everything to its' fullest, and loving everything intensely. Pure rejoicing is not good either. If you purely love everything you develop a dependency, a neediness, and when you don't have the thing that you are in love with you freak out. You are unstable. Pure detachment protects you from ever freaking out but you're autistic, you don't ever really feel anything. A nice balance of the two practices would be to enjoy things deeply but not to need them. Practice the art of being willing to go without it. The word 'willing' is so key. You don't actually have to go without things in life as long as you are willing to. If, in your heart, you are willing to go without it, you have broken any possible fear that is attached to the issue.

Fear is our belief that we need something and we may not get it. A jealous person thinks they need their partner and they are afraid of losing their partner. That is a quick way to ruin a relationship, to need it. It's not realistic. It's not spiritual. It's fear-based. If you are willing to go without something, to let it go, then love, spiritual energy naturally flows and you don't end up losing it. The partner loves you all the more. This is probably the great paradox of life; if you need something you will ruin it and you will cause yourself to go without it. If you are willing to go without it, it will tend to come to you. Fear ruins things. If we do things fearfully, we tend to mess it up.

Try this for any job interview, before you go in meditate and practice not needing the job.

Be careful, when I say practice not needing the job, it doesn't mean you don't enjoy it. Balance this by thinking, "It would be nice to have this job. What a nice place to work, but there are other jobs. I'll be alright. The Higher Power will provide. If it works out, that's great, and if not it was pleasant to meet everyone here." Go into a job interview with that kind of balanced attitude. You would enjoy the job, but you don't need it. You will have a mature, spiritual, balanced, comfortable disposition and your chances of getting the job have greatly increased. If you go in with fear and neediness, or total detachment, those extremes won't help you.

Practice these things in your everyday life. I had a Buddhist friend and he was eccentric. He would apply the principle of detaching throughout his day. He practiced being willing to die, and willing to go without things. He didn't have a TV in his home and I offered him a TV once. He said, "No thank you, TV just gets you attached to things telling you to buy, buy, buy. It's just capitalism trying to seduce you into believing you need everything." When he would go to Walmart and before he would put anything in his cart, he would stop for a few seconds and ponder if he really needed the item. If he decided he did need it, he would put it back and practice going without it. He would only let himself have it after he learned not to need it.

All you really need is your higher power. You don't even need air. If your body died, your spirit would still be standing there eternal as ever. You don't even need air, or a body, you don't even need this earth. The attitude of not needing things is a realistic perspective. It's the highest spiritual perspective that you can get. Practice this throughout your day. Anytime you start to feel anxious take a moment and think about what it is that you perceive that you need. You are anxious because you think you need something, you've become too attached to it. Practice telling yourself, "I'm going to trust my higher power. However things work out is going to be fine, even if it hurts. It will be a good lesson." It's not an easy path, but daily practice will help you become stronger and stronger at it.

The enemy of our soul mainly works through our fears. It can't physically hurt you, it can only put energy into you in the forms of feelings or thoughts. The thoughts are always a fear driving you to attachment. Fear that makes you believe that you need something. It starts out as a fear and it tries to get you to cling to a defense in order to hide from the fear. Fear makes us extreme. If we are afraid of the right, we run too far to the left. We go to the extreme because we want to attach to something that provides us some kind of safety. We want to attach to something that gives us real comfort. You can come to the attitude that you don't need that defense, you don't need that comfort. If you exercise that kind of faith and detachment, the enemy can't get you to react to the extreme. Extremism is terrible for us. Extremism throws all of the systems of your body and soul off-balance. Extremism is unrealistic, you don't fit life. Extremism is annoying, no one wants to be around you. Extremism blocks out God, spiritual energy. Extremism is hiding, not in a cave, but behind some narrow truth or personality trait.

The secret of life is to find out who you really are.

You are one with everything in the Universe. Fear makes us cling to one small aspect of who we really are. Fear prevents us from knowing that we are a divine being that is one with everything in the Universe. It might be our good looks that we cling to. We believe we are a valuable person just because we are pretty. We might think we are valuable because we are good at our profession. You are so much more than your looks, your profession, or any small aspect of your identity. I'll share a quote from Brad Pitt, I was channel surfing the other day and came across his comment that I thought was incredibly enlightening. I really like this guy. This guy has got it all; talent, money, fame, good-looks, a beautiful wife, a beautiful family and he is well liked by the world. The interviewer asked him if he was happy. He answered, "Sometimes. Life is like that, some weeks I'm happy, some weeks I'm not. People get too attached to happiness. They stress out about it." I completely agree with this statement. I teach my clients that life is good if you are happy part of the time, and not happy for part of the time. That's life. It means you have a good amount of challenges going on. It provides us opportunity to daily practice self-comfort, detachment, and faith.

I want to discuss the first rule of war, know your enemy, by knowing what your core fear is.

Remember the list of ten core fears. Think about the fear that rated the highest for you on the scale of one to ten. You really need to know what your main core fear is. Memorize it and how that theme shows up in your life. Most of the challenges that go on in your life, there will be your one core fear hidden in the situation. Your core fear will be driving, and manifesting the situation.   Now that you have your core fear in mind, remember the importance of the battle. The enemy will try to distract us and keep us focused on things that really don't matter. Items of eternal importance should be what we focus on.

How can we get fear out of our bodies so that spiritual energy can flow through us? That is a thought of eternal importance, not worrying about bills, or if your team will win, or what you should wear. The only reason challenges are important in your life is to the degree that it exposes your fear. Everything that you want is due to not getting enough spiritual energy. If you develop this higher source of spiritual energy, this higher source of comfort, the eternal ability to get as much of it as you want then you will naturally let go of your fears and neediness of the things of the world.

Think of the top problems in the world; violence, drug addiction, sexual immorality, divorce, and so on, the biggest problems are just from people who are seeking some source of external comfort. It is not eternal. It doesn't matter. They hide from their fears by seeking some eternal comfort. You need to practice not needing the worldly comforts such as alcohol, bad attitude, sex, food, video games, praise from others, or whatever it is that you rely on for comfort. Those things will help you for a moment but it doesn't last for very long. You need to do your duty and work on the daily practice of internal self-comfort, self-mastery techniques. We'll spend a whole class teaching more about those.

Babies get all of the comfort that they want. There is a saying in parenting training, "You can't spoil a baby." Parenting is a process of taking comforts away from your child as they get older. You take their privileges away. A child might ask for a sandwich and the parent tells them to get it for themselves. The child complains that they don't want to go to school and the parent says, "Oh, cry me a river, you are going to school." Then the teenagers ask for cash to go get something fun and the parent says, "How about you work and earn that money?" That is what God, as our parent, does to us too. As we get older, the comforts we rely on get taken away. Pretty soon we have aches and pains in our bodies. Pretty soon we start to lose our good looks and our spouse loses their good looks. Pretty soon our job gets taken away, you lose your job or retire. Your children grow and move away, it becomes harder and harder to get comfort from the world. Hopefully throughout your life you practice internal comfort and rely on your higher power, on spiritual energy.

In order to do the third rule of war, fight wisely, I want to teach you how to use the Pendulum Theory. It is a nice little map to see what is going on with your fear. One of the hardest things about the fear battle is that it is so invisible and complex. Most people don't ever really understand it. If you can see on this map, where you are on the pendulum, you will have knowledge. Knowledge helps you win the battle. Knowledge is powerful. The Pendulum Theory states that everything in the world has an opposite, so whatever we are afraid of has an opposite. If we are afraid of abandonment, the opposite would be to get really close to a bunch of people and having a lot of support.

People evolve on their path. Like a pendulum, people will swing from one extreme to the opposite extreme. The truth is in the middle. We hope to find and settle into the middle and stop swinging. At first we are at one extreme, then we do a wild swing to the opposite extreme. The next swing will not be quite as extreme, and we swing back and forth until we eventually settle down in the middle. The first stage of our maturity in this battle is that we develop a fear. Stage two is running away from the fear in the opposite direction. We cling desperately to the opposite of our fear. This is why we can discover what someone's fear is just by observing what stands out about them. Whatever they are extreme about is not comfortable for them, it's not natural, but they keep it up to hide from the fear that is in the opposite direction. We need the opposite side, at least in moderation to be balanced, to be whole, to be realistic. This means that we have to go over and make friends with the side we are afraid of. We need to accept some of it, not all of it. One of our defenses is to think in black or white terms. This is how children think. As adults our mind has matured to see that there are shades of grey in all thinking, everything is not black or white. As soon as you get the heart beat racing, and the fear is going, our thinking goes right back to a child.

The only way we can get the pendulum to stop swinging is to accept a moderate amount of the side that you fear.

Now, be careful because the enemy will whisper to you all kinds of extremist thinking. You will be overwhelmed by the experience of your fear so you will be vulnerable to the childlike, black or white, way of thinking. You have to seek moderation. Trust it. Moderation is a great power. Fear drives extremism. All of the evils of the world are extremism. Extremism ruins us, and it ruins the people around us. The middle ground is reality. It is the balance of truth on both sides. It makes you whole.

The second stage, being extreme on some issues, can last your entire lifetime. This is an uncomfortable, dangerous stage that is ruining your life. It is a time bomb that is going to explode eventually and cause traumas over and over and over again. We tend to get stuck in stage two because the only alternative is to go back to the direction that we are afraid of. Fortunately life does us a tremendous favor of traumatizing us when we are extreme. What happens is that extreme behaviors cause bad things to happen in our lives. Those traumas build up over time until you become afraid of your own defense. The side that you are running to, might have been really comfortable when you were younger, but after all of these traumas your new personality trait has become scary to you.

Let me give you an example; a person afraid of rejection so they go around trying to please everybody. The person is pleasing everyone and they are eventually taken for granted, taken advantage of, and treated like trash. That really hurts when it happens over and over again. One day that person goes postal. It happens to moms all of the time. Mom is pleasing everyone and she is taken advantage of, until one day she has had enough and she goes on strike. It is a good thing when a mom gets to this point. It means she has entered stage three; she is not going to be everyone's door mat. Stage three is the swinging of the pendulum. At first it is wild, erratic and chaotic. She swings between the two sides because she is afraid of keeping up the side that keeps traumatizing her so she goes back to the other side, but she is afraid of the other side from her childhood. She's afraid of that extreme, telling people off, so she runs back to pleasing people until it's too much and she swings again. Stage three is very painful because there is nowhere to hide from your fears. Since there is nowhere to hide, you won't be stuck in this stage for very long. This is the stage when people usually come to therapy. They are desperate and scared. They feel like they are losing their mind. They don't know who they are anymore. When I hear this I am glad because I know that they are getting close to enlightenment.

Lao Tzu, the founder of Daoism stated, "The world around me is content. I alone am troubled." The enlightened master said that we must be troubled. This swinging back and forth will cause us to be troubled. We fix it by seeking moderation. When you find yourself swinging toward one of the extremes you practice self-mastery and stop yourself. Encourage yourself to get back to middle ground. It's hard to do. It's such a new thing. It's stressful for the personality. The personality loves habits. When you establish a routine, when you're stuck in the same old same old, your mind is clear. You don't have to process a lot. You are not growing. Enlightenment is troubling because there are a lot of conflicts that you are resolving. The mind should be stretched and strained to a moderate degree.

Consistent, moderate pressure, is my philosophy in life. It is how I treat my children, and myself, with consistent moderate pressure, not too much or too little, and not erratic swings. I tell people that in order to stop the pendulum from swinging, you seek moderation and practice meditation. The swings are caused by discomfort so if you can meditate and bring self-comfort you will be able to stop the swinging. When you are comfortable you won't need the extreme things. The number one reason for drug and alcohol abuse is anxiety. We run to these extremes because we seek comfort. If you meditate you will become naturally moderate and you won't need those defenses. Anxious people are desperate for extremes. In order to find the middle ground you must learn to comfort yourself.

Ask yourself which of these stages you are in with your core fear. Are you stuck on one side, clinging to a defense because you are afraid of the opposite? That is not enlightenment. That is wasting time. Any extreme trait about you, you should go battle against it. You need the opposite side to become a whole human being and the opposite side is something you are afraid of. You've been running from it for years. You need a moderate amount of that opposite side. Are you in the swinging stage, going from one extreme to another? Keep your eye on the prize, settling down in the middle and getting comfortable.

Two important goals you should have are to be moderate and comfortable. It will make you a whole human being with spiritual energy naturally flowing through you.

The Pendulum Theory is very helpful as you battle your core fear on every issue. There are a lot of different pendulum swings happening. There is not just one issue and not just one fear. If we are to fight wisely, consider that before a battle any great general is concerned about what ground you will fight on. In Gettysburg, for example, there was a race to see who got the higher ground, the north got to it first and won the battle. Applying this to our spiritual battle against our fears, be careful not to fight when you have the less favorable ground.

Let me give you an example; let's say you are tired, or have the flu, or you are really stressed out in your life. Is that a good time to go fight your core fear? No, that is the time to rest, heal up, and nurture yourself for a while. One of the greatest self-mastery techniques is to turn your brain off. When it's too hard go get some movies and chill for a while. If your mind is too busy, racing with worries, then it's extreme and driven by fear and you should shut your brain off so you can get your balance. When we are stressed out is when we instinctively want to fight the battle because we seek comfort. We seem to want to fight and talk about things when we are most stressed. It is a terrible time to confront the issue. If go to battle at that time, the enemy has the higher ground. He will have a heyday with you. The chances of winning that battle are slim.

Anyone who has been in a traumatic relationship knows what I'm talking about. When you've had an intense argument, one of those knock-down, drag out, confrontations that lasts for several hours and no one is backing down it is not doing you any good. The enemy is using your core fear to call you to a battle you don't want to fight. Have that conversation when you are more comfortable. Get some sleep, take a hot bath, go for a walk, take a time out, or watch some mindless TV and comfort yourself.   If you fight and work yourself up to a panic attack, then your fear is going to be twice as strong.   You've just traumatized yourself.   This pendulum swing takes time to settle down to the middle.

If we traumatize ourselves, we push it back to the extreme and the process will take longer to resolve.   It's important that as we are seeking balance with our core fear, we avoid being retraumatized.   While you are working on beating your fear you should limit your time with dramatic people and situations. They will retraumatize you. Spend time around mellow, stable, moderate people and your healing will go faster, the pendulum will settle down really quickly.   If you keep doing extreme things and hanging around extreme people the pendulum will continue to swing erratically.

Remember how great the reward is, to be a whole person.

You really love yourself. You love this whole, balanced, energy-channeling person who is comfortable all of the time. You want that. You want that more than anything in the world. It is so important for this life and the next. One of my heros, Oprah, on her 50th birthday after decades of extreme behaviors she finally settled down. She said, "Age has really given me what I've always wanted; myself." She is a billionaire and could have practically anything. She figured out that the most important thing is what her experiences have taught her; how to be comfortable with who she is. She likes herself. She doesn't need anything or anybody and doesn't need to prove anything. She is comfortable in her own skin. Money cannot buy that. Nothing can give this to you but time, and moderating on the pendulum.

If you do have a problem with somebody, make sure you are both comfortable. You can make this very overt, just tell the person, "I've got something that I want to talk to you about. I want to be sure that we're both comfortable because I really want to have a good conversation about it because you are so important to me. When is a good time for you?" If another person comes to you and wants to have a big conversation but you are not comfortable you have a right, a very sacred, important right to say, "Give me some time. I can tell that this is important. I'm a little stressed, I'm going to take a little time and then we can talk later tonight." You can be really direct with people like this. It's very effective. Society is advising young couples never to go to bed mad, that it is bad for their marriage. If it takes sleep and time in order to be comfortable before a big discussion, you should go to bed.

Accept a balance in the situation. Aknowledge that you want to solve the problem, but accept that you only have half of the power to do it. Everything is in balance in this Universe, including our power. We have half power to change our problems and the other half to realize we are stuck with the problem. We are stuck accepting, in moderation, part of the fear that comes up due to the problem. It's a little like dieting. We want to believe that we can have a perfect shape but we need to accept that we don't have all of the power of the Universe. We have half power. We should have moderate expectations. We can change some things, and some things we are stuck with and we accept it. We make friends with some of the fear associated with our body image. It is a good lesson in life. When you are processing a problem with someone and they are willing to meet you half way, it is perfect for you. If you got everything perfectly your way, you would be spoiled. You would be avoiding the fear that the other options represent. In life you get half of what you want, you are in the ideal learning situation.

I became a lot happier once I accepted this.

I was a perfectionist. I was chasing the Disney-like dream, riding off into the sunset with my princess. We want to believe that life is supposed to be happy all of the time. The couples always live happily-ever-after. That is bull. They got home from the honeymoon and someone had to do the dishes, pay the bills, take care of screaming children and they weren't happy about it all of the time. Like Brad Pitt realized, they were happy some weeks and not happy on some weeks. The couple lived 'happily ever...half of the time'. I became a lot happier in my life once I accepted this as my goal. My spouse is really half of what I really want in a spouse.

Excellent. I'm only half of what she really wants. There is no sense expecting our spouse to be on a white horse like Disney said they should be. God does us a big favor by giving us half of what we want. The other half will expose your fears and help you grow.

There are three rules of solving a conflict with somebody.

You have a conflict because both people have their fears involved. It is an incredible opportunity to heal some fears. Whoever wins the conflict doesn't really matter. The only thing that matters while resolving the conflict is that those fears stay moderate and that you don't get re-traumatized. The argument can be an incredible opportunity if you proceed with skill and carefulness, if you follow these three sacred rules. You need these rules, don't try and solve a conflict without them. Resist the temptation to follow your instincts and so something extreme, but follow these rules;

1. **Make sure both people are comfortable.**

2. **Truth is always on both sides, admit that both you and your adversary are both right to some degree.**

3. **Meet in the Middle**

Our fear makes us want to be right. We believe that we are 100% right and they are 100% wrong. Wouldn't it be great to hide that ego trip believing we are superior to the other person?

If we believe that, we will force the issue to get them to believe us and agree with us completely. Truth is you are half-wrong and they are half-right. It's perfect that way. If you cannot see the truth on the other side, at least have faith that it is there. I cannot tell you how many people cannot trust that there is some truth on the other side of each argument. Nobody can hide from their fears in this world because both sides are equally true on every issue. You might feel anxious about this idea because your fears are being stirred. Trust that this process will help you settle your fears and feel comfortable in these situations. It will take practice but it is worth it. You cannot hide from a superior attitude or belief system. If you were traumatized, if somebody abused you, it will be really hard to apply this truth. Your fears will be screaming, "No way!!!"

The hardest time that I have in teaching this principle is when somebody is a victim. Not right away, but eventually on their path I help the victim understand that it is partly their fault. It is a terrible thing to say to a victim. There is power in the understanding that to some degree we manifested the events of our lives. To some degree our fears, our defenses, our extremism manifested that situation. When we take that power over our experiences, we can battle our core fears. Abusers go around looking for people with unresolved fear in them. Abusers avoid people who are confident and comfortable. Abusers want to take their negative energy and put it into somebody for the relief it brings. They seek a target in someone who is fearful and vulnerable and they shove that energy into them by physical or sexual violence and verbal put downs. Our unresolved fears and insecurities make us a target for abuse. Accepting that gives us power to battle the core fear. When we avoid the battle and feel sorry for ourselves for years at a time, we are wasting our time by not working on growth. If we don't resolve the issue, we will cause the fear to play out again. We have the power to attract trauma in our lives, and we have the power to stop the trauma. It would be easy to say, "None of it is my responsibility. I did not contribute to the cycle of abuse." The brave thing to do, the powerful thing to do, is to say, "I've got the power to do something about it. I'm going to train and get some skills. If this happens in my life again I have the power to stop it."

Life is just a series of lessons. As long as we get up every time life experiences bring us down. Life is hard because you are so powerful that you needed hard in order to grow. Your future is so incredibly amazing that you need to pass this hard training. You need a challenge that is equal to your spirit. Don't get too discouraged about this path. Shake it off. We are going to lose some rounds as we fight this battle. No worries.

The third rule of conflict solving is to meet in the middle.

How do you meet in the middle, just cut it in half. That is what our kids do. Two kids are arguing over a cookie they will agree it's fair if they each take half. Almost every argument can find a middle ground. Both people feel respected that way, and both people's fears get comforted. Our fears get worse when we say, "It has to be my way not your way." The other person's ego is really threatened and their fear is twice as strong. If you say, "Look, let's both respect each other so let's meet in the middle." The fears just calm down. No one is going to get more than the other. No one is superior to the other. No one will feel disrespected or put down. There is no re-traumatizing of fears. You have to be tough about this if they push the issue. You can say, "I can meet you in the middle. That is the best I can do. It is fair. If I meet you totally your way then I'm a door mat. If I meet totally my way then I'm a jerk, a hard ass. If I meet you in the middle I'm a reasonable, respectful human being. That is all I will do for you, meet you in the middle." You might have to repeat yourself. It might take them hearing it a few times before they believe that you mean it. I believe in a baseball policy, give them three strikes. Offer them the middle ground three times and if they don't accept by the third time you withdraw the offer because they cannot have a reasonable conversation. Get out of there. There is no sense talking with such a fear-driven animal. Get away from an extremist, fearful, dangerous, abusive personality who is not willing to meet in the middle. Those are people you don't want to be around. They take all their fear and negative energy from their life history and they are trying to give it to you. If they do accept the middle ground, you can shake hands over the issue. Over the long run you will see that it is good for the relationship. Being on equal ground, showing respect for one another is a good foundation for a healthy relationship.

This battle is so important. Keep practicing consistent, moderate pressure on this stuff. Don't be an extremist and try to be perfect about it. It will just make your fears worse. Laugh at your fears a little bit. Realize that you will win some battles and lose some battles but if you keep training you will find the balance, peace, and comfort you deserve.

Thank you very much for learning with me.

The other books in Mark Kailing's Self Mastery Lecture Series:

Purpose of Life

Law of Integration

The Gender War

Battling Core Fears

Deeper Relationships

The Dark Side of Relationships

Map of the Mind

A Profoundly Open Mind

Lifelong Path of Grace

What We Now Know

Improve your Mental Health by Improving your Physical Health

Self-Mastery and Religion

Overcome Your Core Fears

Your Spiritual Path